WOMAN TO WOMAN

ABORTION -VS-BIOLOGICAL CLOCK

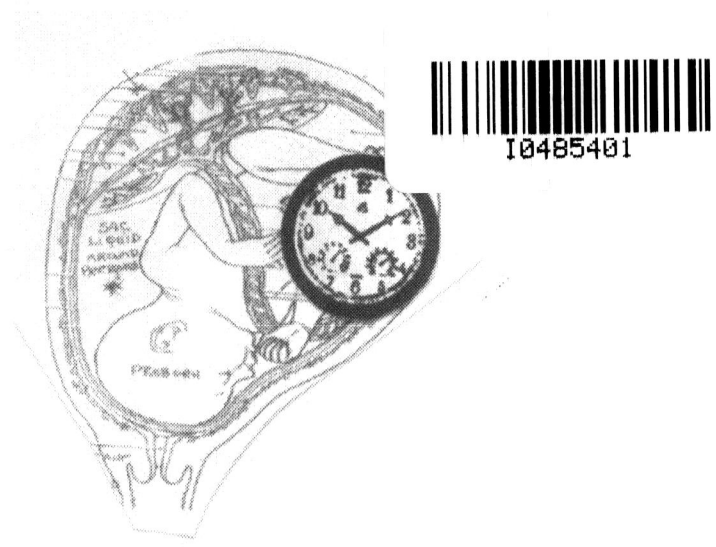

THE ABORTION COVER-UP !

By: A. Komorowski

Note for Librarians: A cataloguing record for this book is available from Library and Archives Canada at www.collectionscanada.ca/amicus/index-e.html
ISBN 1-4120-8629-9

Printed on paper with minimum 30% recycled fibre.
Trafford's print shop runs on "green energy" from solar, wind and other environmentally-friendly power sources.

Offices in Canada, USA, Ireland and UK

Book sales for North America and international:
Trafford Publishing, 6E–2333 Government St.,
Victoria, BC V8T 4P4 CANADA
phone 250 383 6864 (toll-free 1 888 232 4444)
fax 250 383 6804; email to orders@trafford.com
Book sales in Europe:
Trafford Publishing (UK) Limited, 9 Park End Street, 2nd Floor
Oxford, UK OX1 1HH UNITED KINGDOM
phone 44 (0)1865 722 113 (local rate 0845 230 9601)
facsimile 44 (0)1865 722 868; info.uk@trafford.com
Order online at:
trafford.com/06-0385

10 9 8 7 6 5 4 3

<u>DEDICATION</u>

I want to dedicate this book to my late husband, Joseph, who gave me the incentive to write. He was my inspiration, my joy, and my best friend.

CONTENTS

ILLUSTRATIONS

WOMAN TO WOMAN

(ABORTION VS. THE BIOLOGICAL CLOCK)

By Anne Komorowski

INTRODUCTION

This book is written to point out the complications that could occur to a woman when she decides to have an induced abortion. What happens when a woman goes against the biological clock of nature? It is important that women understand, you cannot stop the clock (cycle of pregnancy) abruptly, by having an abortion, terminating the pregnancy, and not expect repercussions from it.

Your body is not programmed to do anything different other than complete the cycle of pregnancy. When you have an induced abortion, it puts a glitch in the natural birth cycle Your body responds to an induced abortion, by malfunctioning, possibly leading to any number of serious complications.

Where will it occur in the body and when? During the abortion or after the abortion? The complication could occur years after, as far as menopause. The following pages will explain the different complications a woman must contend with. The question is, can she endure, them, because she had a choice, a choice, without the knowledge of not knowing, whether it was a safe choice.

NOTE: The terminology, embryo and fetus are used by the medical field. My preference is using the term unborn baby.

1

CHAPTER 1.

THE TRUTH ABOUT ABORTION!
(Is there a Cover-up?)

As you know the United States Supreme Court has legalized abortion in 1973. This move has given a woman the right to choose to continue her pregnancy, or to have an induced abortion.

Over 30 years of legal abortion, there are still many controversial arguments about abortion. The bottom line of these arguments should be **"how safe is it for a pregnant woman to have an abortion"?**

This book is meant to be informative and educational. Besides having the right to make a choice, a woman has the right to know when she chooses to have an abortion, she is facing over 100 potential complications. Teenagers are afflicted with the highest amount of these complications, the worst complication of all, the *climax of death!*

Understandably, women want control, in the right to choose to be pregnant or to have an abortion, and, in1973, they were given that right. However, the lack of knowledge regarding the consequences of having an abortion, was denied.

Abortion with its' many complications should have been investigated before women were given the green light to have an abortion. Because Mother Nature or the biological clock of a woman's reproductive system, determines when a young girl will enter puberty, when she will begin to develop physically, when she will begin her menstrual cycle, and also, when she becomes sexually active. The biological clock even governs what days of the month she is fertile and when she can become pregnant. When a woman becomes pregnant, she goes through different body changes, in order to prepare for the birth of the baby. And then there's menopause, the last stage of a woman's reproductive cycle.

All these natural changes or the biological clock occur in sequence throughout a woman's life. This biological clock is in complete control and determines the time span for each change in a woman's life. For instance, within nine months, a pregnant woman's body is noticeably changing and adapting itself, to prepare for the birth of a baby. In the meantime, having an abortion, causes an abrupt change, in the sequence of the pregnancy cycle. You cannot interrupt this natural process with a violent act like induced abortion, nor control this natural process of child birth and not expect complications from it.

Logic prevails here, not some fantasy or illusion that a woman can control her body. Understandably control, to some women, may mean 'control of choice' rather than 'control of body'. Think about it! A woman really has no say when it comes to the biological functions of child birth and of her body. Abortion's procedure is an intrusion and a traumatic shock, to the pregnant woman's body, physically, mentally and emotionally.

Women have been led to believe that having an abortion is safe, a simple solution, but many times, abortion is being used, as a means to end an unwanted pregnancy, or to avoid men's financial responsibility. What has not been told, openly and honestly, is the fact, that having an induced abortion, is not easy, nor is it simple, or safer than child birth, or any other medical procedure. Induced abortion is far from safe, especially when it's used against childbirth, a natural function, and which is governed, by a biological clock. The lack of knowledge about induced abortion, and its' many complications and the safety issues of a pregnancy should be a woman's priority. One priority should be to teach young girls about induced abortion and about complications that can derive from having an abortion. Abortion and its' complications should be included in the school's curriculum. The next priority should be that women learn about abortion and all its' tragic outcomes before they have an abortion.

The only way that legal abortion could be considered safe, is the fact, that it is safer than illegal abortion, because emergency medication and/or equipment, have become available, to the woman without criminal investigation. A pregnant woman is not equipped with an instant shut-off mechanism nor is there a magical man-made procedure that will return her body back to normal functions after she has had an induced abortion. What does induced abortion mean? It is a forced, unnatural procedure perpetrated on a woman's body, or more specifically, on her reproductive system. An induced abortion leaves a pregnant woman with an unfinished birth cycle.

This unfinished birth cycle must find an avenue to complete itself. As you know the woman's body is not meant to perform any other function during the birth cycle other than prepare for the arrival of the pregnant woman's baby.

After conception, a woman's psychological makeup, her reproductive organs or any other parts of her body functions are governed by the biological clock. A woman's body functions are not programmed, equipped or designed, in any way, to deal with an abrupt interruption, such as induced abortion. Unfortunately a sudden interruption of a pregnant woman's birth cycle will cause a malfunction in her body, but the question is, "how and where in the woman's reproductive system or elsewhere in her body will this malfunction occur"? "Will the malfunction take place immediately during the abortion, or in the form of a failed abortion, or with a terrible reaction to one of the powerful drugs used during the abortion procedure"? It may happen during the abortion procedure, or a few days later after the abortion, when possible hemorrhaging may occur along with an infection. Or perhaps later in life when a woman enters menopause. And then there's the stress factor, which causes other illnesses, depending how great the stress is. Breast cancer is also looked upon as a possible repercussion of having an abortion. There are many questions that need to be answered by experts, who are honest and caring. Also, it should be emphasized,   that abortion and it's procedures have not been investigated or documented sufficiently. Plus, it is not discussed openly enough. Many people consider an abortion as a hush-hush matter, or it's too emotional to discuss.

It is a known fact that teenagers' reproductive systems do not fully mature until they are about twenty-five years old. If that's true then that could be the reason why teenagers are having the so many complications.

Perhaps it is time to look at induced abortion another way. The plain fact is that, abortion is a business for profit, like any other money-making business, except that women, in this case, are the victims of this profit. Part of the cover-up, is women and young girls, have been misled, to believe induced abortion is simple, safe and uncomplicated, with no side effects. Besides this intrusion, known as abortion, upon a natural wonder, known as child birth, a woman must contend with doctor-made-errors, such as punctures and/or tears in her reproductive organs during the abortion procedure. These 'doctor-made mistakes', plain carelessness, or even accidental mishaps, can lead to sterility for the woman aborting, never more to have a future baby of her own. This is one of the worst dilemmas for a young woman to contend with.   .

Furthermore, women are misled into the fantasy that having an induced abortion, is the answer, to an unwanted, unexpected pregnancy, and that induced abortion is safe, with no repercussions. Perhaps one reasons why women are misled in thinking that induced abortion is safe, because there are lack of records, showing all the complications and fatalities, that are occurring, from an induced abortion.

Hospitals are required, to have necessary life-saving equipment, should an emergency arise. Clinics do not! Hospitals must keep accurate records and employ licensed, skilled professionals. Clinics do not! Also, hospitals must report deaths, resulting from complications. Clinics, without having to adhere, to state regulations, operate with a free-hand policy. Hospitals are regulated and are answerable, for their actions. Clinics operate without restrictions or government guidelines to follow.

Because of no regulations, no one to account to officially, abortion has become a lucrative and highly profitable business involving billions of dollars!

There should be greater concern about the "free hand" that abortion clinics operate with, rather, than freedom of choice or control of one's body. Yes, freedom of choice is awesome, but control of one's body is an impossibility. When a young girl goes from adolescence to puberty (child bearing), she is governed by a biological clock in her reproductive system. When a woman has conceived and becomes pregnant, she again, is governed by the biological clock. This natural clock determines when the baby completes its' growth cycle, and is ready to be born.

A miscarriage is a natural way of protecting the mother, when the babies' growth, is not functioning properly, or is dead in her uterus. This natural body rejection, unlike induced abortion, where the doctor, must use drugs and surgical equipment to remove the baby. The big difference here, is that the baby is dead when a miscarriage occurs, but the baby is alive, at the beginning of an induced abortion, then, put to death, by the abortionist.

The decision was made to legalize abortion, but the abortion procedure was not, thoroughly investigated, to ensure the safety of pregnant women. It should have been ascertained exactly how an induced abortion, can affect a woman, physically, psychologically, or emotionally, and to what extent?

The national abortion decision was built, on the judicial fact that abortion was to be a health service to women, should her pregnancy be life-threatening. Or if the unborn baby was handicapped in any way, and to halt child abuse, or by acts of rape or incest. Plus, abortion was legalized, to reduce the number of teenage pregnancies. But today, instead of health reasons, abortion in most cases, has become a form of birth control, and relief from financial responsibility. Initially, one reason abortion was legalized, was that it would stop the epidemic of unwanted teenage pregnancies. It's not working because the number of pregnancies among teenagers is still staggering. As long as society gives mixed messages about sex to teens, the pregnancies are not going to stop.

From the ages of 11 to 19 account for about one-fourth of all induced abortions, then young women between the ages of 20 to 24 account for one-third percent. The combination of the two young ages, totals more than one-half of the induced abortions that occur in this country. Sadly, these two age groups are the ones who are afflicted, with the highest amount of complications and fatalities, from having an induced abortion.

Furthermore, abortion was legalized to prevent child abuse. It didn't and it doesn't, and the griping fact, shows that child abuse has become worse. Since the legalization of abortion, child abuse is up over 1,000%. The traumatic ordeal of an abortion, itself, can leave a woman, with the feeling of low self-esteem, and the inability to cope with stress, which are the two (2) major factors, that contribute to the cause of child abuse.

Another reason abortion was legalized, was to eliminate birth defects. This may be a sound reason, but, the other side of the coin, is that, chances are extremely greater for a woman, to give birth to a wanted baby, who may be born handicapped or crippled anyway, due to having an abortion in the first place.

Logically, if having an induced abortion, increases your chances of having handicapped and/or deformed babies in future wanted pregnancies, then the reasoning here, is that an abortion is not a good choice.

Finally, induced abortion was legalized to slow down the population growth. Since sterility is so high on the list of complications, the possible retardation of the population growth, has been definitely accomplished, by having an induced abortion.

CHAPTER 2.

METHODS OF ABORTION

WHICH ONE WILL YOU CHOOSE?

Choosing which method to be used to abort your unborn baby will depend how far along you are in your pregnancy. There are six (6) surgical methods used for inducing termination of your pregnancy, one partial birth method, and two (2) medical abortions, that basically uses drugs to abort.

1. SUCTION ASPIRATION METHOD

It is used in 95% of induced abortions. Since induced abortion is an unnatural procedure, an intrusion used upon a natural condition as pregnancy, the cervix has to be forced open. The cervix, a little known organ is sometimes referred to as the neck of the uterus. It is a very important part of your reproductive system. It is closed very securely to hold the unborn baby and fluid in the mother's uterus. When the unborn baby is at full term, the cervix will naturally open or dilate in the form of contractions. Normally, the cervix does not dilate ahead of schedule. It stays tightly closed for the protection of the unborn baby. Therefore it has to be forced open when a woman is aborting. This, is done, by first inserting a slender steel rod, then a thicker one, into the cervix to pry it open. In the meantime a larger rod with a hook-like end is put through the cervix to keep it open.

Then a powerful suction tube is inserted into the uterus through the forced, held open cervix. The power of the suction tube is 29 times more powerful than a common household vacuum sweeper. This suction tube sucks the unborn baby from the uterus (incidentally the baby should be dead, but many times it isn't), and then rips the attached placenta (after birth) from the uterus, sucking them into a container. Great care must be used so that no parts of the unborn baby, or the after birth are left in the uterus. If, perchance, any parts are left in the mother's uterus, and if they are not discovered soon enough, a woman can go into shock, and may need a blood transfusion.

Additional surgery may be necessary to remove the uterus. Removal of the uterus may be the only way to stop the bleeding. Unfortunately this way used to stop the bleeding, also can make a woman sterile, unable to have wanted babies in the future.

2. DILATATION AND CURETTAGE METHOD

In this method, the cervix is dilated or stretched, to permit insertion of a loop-shaped steel knife, in order to scrape the wall of the uterus.

The abortionist in this procedure cuts the unborn baby's body in to pieces; plus, cuts the after birth that is attached to the uterus wall. Bleeding is extreme and could cause the woman to hemorrhage. This may, also, result in the removal of the mother's uterus in order to stop the bleeding and to save the mother's life. Non-hospital abortion facilities (clinics) lack blood banks, trained medical staff skilled in resuscitation or surgical facilities, to deal with emergencies. It has been speculated that the risk of death and other serious complications, could be higher than presently surmised, because abortion clinics are not equipped as they should be. The reason, that many clinics are not equipped, as they should be, is because there are very few laws governing abortion facilities. They literally have a "free hand" in operating these facilities. It cannot be emphasized enough, when a pregnant

10

woman is poked and prodded, in an area as vital as the cervix, she will experience repercussions. This method is used primarily during the seventh to the twelfth week of pregnancy. (NOTE) Induced abortion is not a fast or simple procedure, in fact, the time element to expand the cervix takes several hours; anywhere, from ten to seventy-two hours (3 days). The time is needed for effectiveness, and can be very painful and uncomfortable. Also, during this prolonged time, bacteria is likely to multiply, causing a very serious problem, to the mother, known as an infection, which can and will spread quickly throughout the mother's body. If infection goes undetected, chances are that it could lead to a life and death situation.

Infection is the major cause of death associated with legal abortion in the United States.

3. DILATATION AND EVACUATION METHOD

This method is used to remove an unborn baby from the uterus at eighteen (18) weeks, or the second trimester. This method is similar to the Dilatation and Curettage Method (No.2). The difference is that an instrument, known as a forceps, is used to grasp part of the developing unborn baby, who by now has formed bones and cartilage. This is a gruesome task because the unborn baby's skull must be crushed and other body parts must be torn from the mother's uterus. Also, the placenta or after birth is removed. Bleeding in this method is very profuse. Again this method is a great risk to the mother. Hemorrhaging could project exploratory surgery, plus the removal of the mother's uterus may be necessary to save her life. The prognosis is the inability of having another baby ever again.

4. SALINE METHOD (SALT POISONING)

This method is used after sixteen (16) weeks, or the second trimester of the pregnancy when there is enough fluid in the sac surrounding the unborn baby. A needle is inserted through the mother's abdomen directly into the sac, and a solution of concentrated salt is injected into it. The unborn baby breathes in, swallowing the salt and in about one hour of agonizing thrashing about in the mother's uterus, dies from salt poisoning. Then the mother should go into labor, approximately twenty-four (24) hours later, delivering the dead, salt-burned and shriveled-up baby. This is done with great pain, for both, the unborn baby and the mother.

The most feared, potentially fatal complication of the saline method used in abortion, is when an excessive amount of salt is used; besides killing the unborn baby, it can enter into the mother's blood stream. It causes harsh headaches, dry mouths and thirst, numbness and tingling of the fingers; in general, the overall feeling of burning up.

A woman can develop a urinary tract infection, which causes the failure of the uterus to contract. This is important in future wanted pregnancies. This method also, causes dizziness, vomiting, convulsions, brain damage, coma and death.

(NOTE) This method is outlawed in Japan and other countries because they recognize the many complications that could lead to death, or life-long complications to the mother.

In the United States the Saline (Salt Poisoning) Method was the second most used method of inducing abortion. The Saline and Prostaglandin methods are not being used as of late, because too many unborn babies have survived these abortion procedures. And a second induced abortion must take place.

**These babies are the result of a Saline Abortion,
and who died with excruciating pain**

<u>5. PROSTAGLANDINS METHOD</u>

Prostaglandins are hormones, and injecting a concentrated form of these hormones into the sac surrounding the unborn baby, induces violent labor and premature birth, of the unborn baby. Salt or another toxin is first injected into the mother's body to assure that the unborn baby will be delivered dead. This is done because some unborn babies have survived the trauma of prostaglandin birth and have been delivered alive. This method is used during the second half of the pregnancy. The side effects and/or complications resulting from the prostaglandin method can include cardiac arrest (heart failure) and/or rupture of the mother's uterus. Seventy (70%) percent of women suffer from pain and severe abdominal cramps, even with the aid of pain killing drugs. Other side effects are nausea, vomiting, gastrointestinal disturbance and diarrhea despite having been given medication to prevent this.

6. HYSTEROTOMY METHOD

This method is used if the saline or prostaglandin (Nos. 4 & 5) methods do not work. It is similar to the major surgery, known as Cesarean Section or C-Section.

DILATION AND EXTRACTION
(a.k.a. PARTIAL BIRTH ABORTION)

The medical drawings following depict the partial-birth abortion procedure. Partial birth abortion is not the medical term, the medical term is known as Dilation and Extraction (D&Xs). However, partial birth abortion, is a term, that is now acceptable.

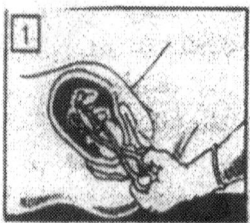

Guided by ultrasound, the abortionist grabs the baby's leg with forceps.

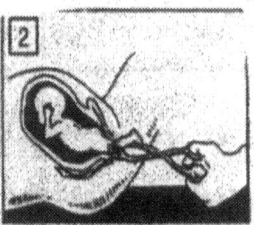

The baby's leg is pulled out into the birth canal.

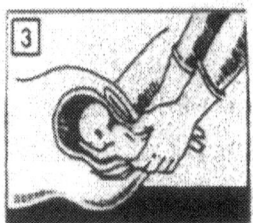

The abortionist delivers the baby's entire body, except for the head.

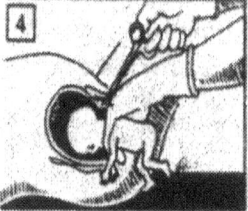

The abortionist jams scissors into the baby's skull. The scissors are then opened to enlarge the hole.

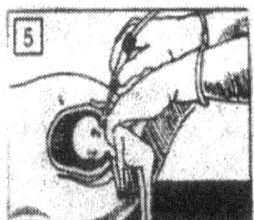

The scissors are removed and a suction tube is inserted. The child's brains are sucked out causing the skull to collapse.

14

The medical drawings have been validated as technically accurate by medical experts on both sides of the abortion issue. The partial birth abortion procedure is used after 20 weeks into the pregnancy, or 4-1/2 to 6 months and later. The cervix is dilated and the unborn baby is delivered feet first; it is then removed up to the neck, from the uterus, then, as you see in the drawing, a pair of scissors are poked in the back of the head. Next, the baby's brains are sucked out of its' head, by a vacuum device, so the head can collapse. By collapsing the head, it is supposed, to make it easier for the abortionist, to remove the unborn baby from the uterus.

Thereby the Pro-choice advocates and/or abortionists alleging state that less damage occurs to the mother's cervix. But the truth of the matter, is that the unborn baby must be killed before it entirely leaves the mother's womb. Why? It could be that there is a law on the books, that when the unborn baby leaves the mother's uterus completely, and is alive and takes its first breath, then the mother, abortionist and his/her assistants could be charged with murder in the first degree! Here is something else, to think about, when a pregnant women is involved in a automobile accident, or any other mishap, and is killed by the carelessness of another person. This person, is then, charged with manslaughter on two accounts, mother and unborn baby. If a crime happens, and the mother's life is taken, the perpetrator when caught and arrested, is charged with two accounts of aggravated murder.

Now when a woman is getting an induced abortion, interestingly enough, she is ridding herself, of a non-viable fetus, not an unborn baby. Which is it? It sounds like double standards of legal rhetoric!

Rather than repeat the horrible facts about partial birth abortion and how its done, the photograph on the preceding page should be suffice in explanation, as to how the partial birth abortion procedure is performed. However, a reminder, is in order once again it must be said, that no matter how advanced medical technology is today, you still can not interrupt the biological clock of the reproductive and not expect a back lash from it.

"Is poking a hole into a helpless baby's head, with a sharp instrument, and sucking out it's brains, called updated medical technology?" Do you wonder what happens to the baby's dead body? Did you ever hear of a heavy duty garbage disposal? Also, research laboratories probably get their share of baby bodies to help with medical research. life, one of the most precious gifts that a man or woman or a child could possess, is looked upon, with such casual disregard.

All the complications, whether minor or major, that women can acquire, by having an induced abortion, indicates that she should make her choice very carefully. Becoming sterile, or by facing the worst complication of all, death to the mother, along with her baby , are not gratifying results, in the matter of having a legal "choice". A *"safe choice "* would be best.

BELOW SHOWS ORGANS OF A WOMAN THAT CAN BE DAMAGED AS A RESULT OF AN ABORTION!

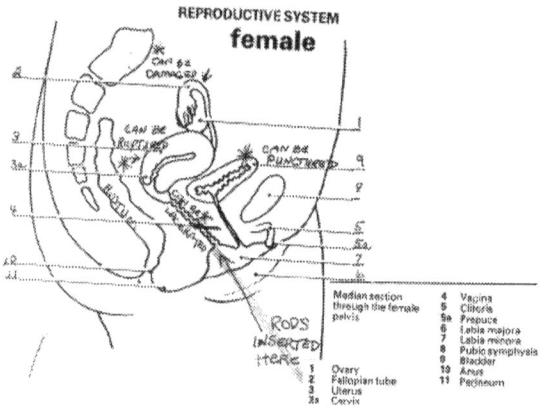

Other damage that occurs due to the use of loop-shaped steel knife, for instance, lacerations to the cervix and the uterus walls. Extreme force is necessary, which could possibly result in profuse bleeding and infections, if not detected soon enough could bring immediate death. Rods are pushed with such force has punctured some women as far as the abdomen. Even kidneys and bowels can be damaged.

SOME AFTEREFFECTS OF ABORTION!

Depression*Feelings of Shame-Low Self-Esteem-Grief-Perforation of the Uterus-Cervical Lacerations-Anxiety Attacks-Uncontrollable Rage-Alcoholism-Suicides-Pain during Sex-Sterility-Death-Loss of Concentration-Embolism-Self-dislike-Chronic Crying-Child Abuse Convulsions-Urinary Tract Damage-Bleeding-Broken Relationships Divorce-Flashbacks when Using Vacuum Sweeper-Anniversary Date-Heart Attacks-Intense Loneliness-Difficulty-Bonding with other Children-Miscarriages-Infections-Bigger risk of bearing Handicapped Children-Drug Addiction-Menstrual Problems-Eating Disorders-Cancer-Nightmares-Unable to Sleep-Anxiety Attacks Emotional Problems-Placenta Previa-Perforated Stomach or other Organs-Cervix Damage unable to function in future pregnancies-Despair-Loss of Concentration-Unable to Sexuality to Perform.

As you can see abortion may not be the best choice or the safest.

MORE DAMAGES BELOW

Rod pushed with such force
has punctured some woman as
far up as the abdomen.

Even kidney
have been
damaged

Bowels can be damaged
(torn) by steel rod.

Uterus.

Preborn Baby

Sac Fluid.

Vagina - susceptible
to infection.

WOMAN'S
REPRODUCTIVE
SYSTEM

Cervix

CHAPTER 3.

QUESTION: WHAT IS RU-486? (a.k.a. Mifepristone)

ANSWER: It is a powerful synthetic steroid, used to induce abortion between the fifth and seventh weeks of pregnancy. It is used with a prostaglandin which induces contractions to occur and it is used to kill unborn babies, and if not closely supervised by a doctor, it, also kills babies' mothers.

Shockingly it is true, let me explain how the RU-486 synthetic steroid technique works, in conjunction with a woman's body. It inhibits the action, of the female hormone progesterone, (an anti-hormone), which means the unborn baby literally starves to death as the nutrient lining of the womb sheds off, and the muscular contractions cause the dead, unborn baby to be discharged from the uterus. If the RU-486 is not successful, then some women will need a suction abortion, either, because of excessive bleeding, or because of an incomplete abortion.

There are three steps in the process of a medical abortion. STEP ONE: A medical history is taken, and a clinical exam, with lab tests are performed. Next, counseling is completed, and informed consent is obtained. If eligible for medical abortion, the women, is then given the RU-486 to swallow. STEP TWO: This step takes place about two days after STEP ONE. Unless the abortion has not occurred and this has been confirmed, by the clinician, the next step, is the woman will then use a drug called misoprostol. These tablets may be swallowed or inserted into the vagina, depending on the treatment regimen of the clinician. STEP THREE: At the office or clinic, this step takes place 10 to18 days after STEP TWO. The clinician evaluates the woman to confirm a complete abortion. It is essential for women to return to the office/clinic, to confirm, that the abortion is complete. If there is an ongoing pregnancy, a suction abortion should be performed. If there is an incomplete abortion, the clinician, should discuss possible alternatives, with the woman.

When the synthetic steroid drug RU 486, is taken alone, only three percent (3%) of woman experience a complete abortion. All other women must take a second potent drug, called prostaglandin. Prostaglandin as you may recall, is accompanied by numerous problems of their own, including potentially lethal side effects, in other words, you can die. In one out of twenty times, the unborn baby, is not killed. The deformities that escalate are so great, that often times, litigation (a lawsuit) is feared, and women are required, to sign an agreement to allow a surgical abortion should the RU-486 method fails. The RU 486/prostaglandin procedure takes three to five days. When heavy bleeding occurs, the average time of bleeding, is about ten (10) days, but some women bleed, as long as thirty (30) days, sometimes longer. It has been reported that five of every one hundred (100) women, bleed so profusely, that surgery is required, to stop the bleeding.

Obviously, some women will require blood transfusions. This profuse bleeding, may lead into a cardiac arrest (heart failure) and consequently death. Other side effects a woman can undergo are (1) severe cramps, (2) nausea, (3) diarrhea, (4) headache, (5) skin rash and (6) vomiting. These are the usual side effects of RU 486. Sometimes women can cope well enough with these side effects when given other medication, providing this medication works.

What are further dangers to women using RU 486? For one, extended heavy internal bleeding can occur, besides the regular heavy bleeding. Remember clinics may not be equipped with the necessary life-saving equipment; so you would have to be transferred to a hospital to receive blood transfusions, if necessary. Internal bleeding may, in a very short time, lead to hemorrhaging, which, then, can become a life and death situation.

Furthermore, the drug RU 486, at times fails to kill the developing unborn baby; thus creating the need for follow-up surgery. Women that smoke and are over the age of 35, may not take RU 486, in France.

At this stage, the pregnant woman, could have second thoughts and decide to continue with the pregnancy, but after taking the powerful drugs, there is no turning back. The question is "if it were possible to reverse the situation, just what bodily condition would her baby be in at the time of normal delivery?" Probably deformed or maimed, because she has ingested a very powerful drug, with dangerous side effects; a drug whose function is to kill. When this drug is administered into the pregnant woman, it is a crucial moment for her unborn baby, since this is the time when the arms, legs and major organs are being formed.

If women are under the impression that RU-486, is a replacement, to an abortion without surgery. Guess again! If a drug with lethal side effects are given to an expectant mother, chances of surgery, are likely, especially, if the woman begins to hemorrhage. Sometimes the only way to stop this heavy bleeding, is to remove the woman's uterus, which then will leave her sterile, never again, to have a wanted baby. Medical abortion, is best done earlier, in the pregnancy. After seven weeks into the pregnancy, then surgical abortion is performed.

Methotrexate (MTX) has been used in the United States, since 1953. It was approved, by the FDA to treat certain types of cancer, but was not approved by the FDA for abortions. Although the FDA did not consider methotrexate for this specific purpose, clinicians may prescribe methotrexate for an early abortion. It can be taken, in the form of an injection, or can be taken orally. Methotrexate and Mifepristone (RU-486) work in different ways.

Methotrexate stops the ongoing implantation process, that occurs during the first several weeks after conception. Mifepristone works by blocking the hormone progesterone, which is necessary to sustain a pregnancy. Without this hormone, the lining of the uterus breaks down, the cervix, the opening of the uterus, softens and bleeding begins. A few days later, after taking either drug, a second drug, misoprostol, is taken. These tablets, which can taken orally, or put into the vagina, which causes the uterus to contract and empty. This ends the pregnancy.

Medical induced abortions take any where from three days to three to four weeks, and require a minimum, of two visits to the clinic. These return visits are very important, since there is no other way to be sure that the abortion has been completed. With methotrexate, about 85% of women will abort in two weeks. Some will take longer and may need more doses of misoprostol. With mifepristone, about 95% of women will abort within two weeks. About one in 20 women who try medical abortion will need, to have a surgical abortion, because the medication does not work for her.

The side effects may include cramps similar to those with a heavy menstrual period, headache, nausea, vomiting, diarrhea, and heavy bleeding. The amount of bleeding will be greater with medical induced abortion, than with surgical induced abortion. Most women have cramps for several hours, and may pass blood clots as they are aborting. Cramps may ease when the unborn baby has passed, but bleeding may last for one to two weeks after a medical induced abortion has been performed.

One complication is that medical induced abortion is irreversible once the drug is taken. So deciding to continue the pregnancy term is not a option at any point after taking the first medication. The other complication is if the unborn baby is not expelled after using these medications, a suction procedure or surgical abortion must be done to empty the uterus and complete the abortion.

The most common crisis-type complication, of a medical induced Abortion, is heavy bleeding, otherwise, known as disseminated intravascular coagulopathy. This means the woman's blood does not

Clot, so bleeding becomes uncontrollable and life threatening. For this reason, a woman must have access to a telephone and transportation to a hospital, in case emergency treatment is needed. Just like surgical induced abortion, treatment for heavy bleeding might require a D & C. Just like the surgical induced abortion, this procedure, can lead to sterility.

CHAPTER 4.

ECTOPIC PREGNANCY

A pregnancy becomes an ectopic, (a.k.a. tubal) pregnancy when scars form, following a pregnancy terminated by induced abortion. After an abortion, you are up to twenty (20) times more likely to have an ectopic pregnancy.

This pregnancy can cause the next unborn baby to fasten itself outside of the uterus or womb, perhaps, in the fallopian tube or some other unlikely spot, anywhere but uterus, the natural habitat of the baby. The scarring has made the uterus unsuitable and impossible for the baby to enter the uterus naturally. Emergency surgery is normally necessary, to quickly remove the embryo, in order to prevent massive loss of blood, and this, possibly, could cause death to the woman.

In an abortion procedure a doctor may not realize that the baby is developing in the fallopian tube. The abortion will fail and this tubal pregnancy could rupture and emergency surgery must be done to save your life. An ectopic pregnancy may, also, cause death from rupture. All women, in their first trimester, should have an ultrasound to make sure they do not have an ectopic pregnancy.

In addition, to the risk of sterility, women who acquire post-aboral related infections, are five to eight times more likely, to experience ectopic pregnancies. In a 10-year span, the rate of ectopic pregnancies in the United States has risen four-fold. At least 10 to 12 percent, of all maternal deaths, are due to ectopic pregnancy.

CHAPTER 5.

PHYSICAL COMPLICATIONS

The physical problems that can result, from having an induced abortion range, from bleeding internally, (without detection by the abortionist), to hemorrhaging profusely, followed by infection, all which, could lead to sterility and/or death. The death of a mother, especially a young teenage mother, is the most devastating of all physical complications. Realistically any death is devastating.

From the very beginning in the procedure of an induced abortion, complications can brew. First, there are many side effects, from the pain killing drugs and the anesthesia that many pregnant women are subjected to. If the pain killing drugs do not work efficiently, then it can be a very painful time, for the woman aborting. Besides the pain, a woman aborting is generally alone, facing the induced abortion procedure. For the record, anesthesia may stun the baby, within the mother's womb, somewhat, but it does not kill the unborn baby.

Lacerations (tears) of the cervix, is on the top of the list, of a woman's health problems. The cervix, is the organ opening to the mother's uterus, where the unborn baby is located. An induced abortion, is a procedure, that is performed, before a full term pregnancy is complete and, before the cervix is ready to contract or dilate naturally, so it has to be forced to dilate (enlarge or open).

The steel rods inserted into the cervix has to be done, with great, tremendous force and a steady hand. In this part of the abortion procedure, the rod can easily tear the sides of the cervix and cause it to bleed. Even with the utmost care, the cervix can be easily damaged, because it is a very delicate organ of the woman's reproductive system. And the cervix of the teenager, is even more delicate. Remember the cervix is normally closed tight to keep the baby in the uterus. Then, when it's time for the baby to be born, the uterus dilates to expel the baby. In abortion procedure, the doctor must force the cervix open.

Five out of six lacerations or punctures of the cervix occur in teenage girls or women, who never have had a child before. When these punctures occur and should they go undetected, the woman can go into shock from the loss of blood. Internal bleeding is not easily detected. If internal bleeding is undetected, several things could go wrong; for one, the mother could go from minor loss of blood to profuse hemorrhaging instantly. If this emergency is not dealt with immediately, it can become fatal for the mother. Second, if the muscles of the cervix become damaged permanently, these muscles will not be able to support the weight of a baby beyond the third, fourth or fifth month of a wanted future pregnancy. Undoubtedly, it will cause a miscarriage each time the woman gets pregnant. About 1 out of 20 women suffer from lacerations of the cervix. This has caused about 40% increase in miscarriages in women who have had an abortion.

Uterus or uterine perforation (hole through it) necessitates major exploratory abdominal surgery, possible hysterectomy, which generates removal of a woman's reproductive organs. When a woman experiences, physical pain from a second surgery, so close to having an abortion, she faces more emotional trauma. This is devastating for the mother, when she becomes aware of the permanent loss, that she will never have a wanted child in the future. Too many women suffer, from a perforated uterus, which almost always, causes peritonitis, which is an inflamed, infected lining of the abdomen, similar to a ruptured appendix. Also, there is the possibility of retained tissue residue and/or unborn baby parts, that are left in the mother's uterus. This carelessness, can promote infections, which can lead to death quickly, if not detected. Then there's the possibility of damaged organs, plus other conditions such as restlessness, insomnia, chills, fever, uncontrolled bleeding and cramps.

The rupture of the mother's uterus, which results, from being given a drug called 'oxtoacen'. It is used to shorten the length of labor pains. They last anywhere, from 24 to 72 hours, or 1 to 3 days. It is a painful and very stressful time, for the mother, as well as the unborn baby. Scar tissue or adhesions may form, in the healing process and could cause infertility, which means additional surgery. It can cause a miscarriage, tubal or ectopic pregnancies, (outside the uterus), in some women.

The muscular wall of the uterus can be weakened. This is caused by the Saline Method (No. 4) used in abortion procedures. The weakened walls of the uterus, will cause problems, in future wanted pregnancies, by the uterus being unable to house, the unborn baby properly, during the pregnancy.

Infection, is the main cause of death, from having an induced abortion. The time required, for the expansion of the cervix, can be short, as 10 hours, or up to 72 hours, or three days. Time is required for effectiveness, however, this prolonged time necessary, to expand the cervix, allows bacteria, the opportunity to multiply, causing an infection. If the infection is not detected soon enough, it could become hazardous for the mother, in many ways. An infection can appear in the urinary tract, respiratory and vaginal areas. There is, also, infection of the pelvic, genitals and tubal areas.

Infection is not to be looked upon lightly, for it spreads rapidly and if not detected and treated, the bottom line is death. A persistent fever is an important sign of an existing infection. Hepatitis can occur if you have a blood transfusion after an abortion. Plus, placenta previa occurs ten (10) times, more often, after a woman has had an abortion. This is where a future wanted baby's placenta lies on the exit, from the uterus, and this means, that the placenta has to be delivered, or removed, before the baby can get out of the uterus. Circumstances like this, causes the mother to bleed severely, plus the baby can die. However, if the obstetrician foresees this condition, the baby can be saved by Caesarean section.

Some clinics, in order to keep costs down and profits high, do not offer a follow-up examination, after an induced abortion. The abortion industry is a humongous, uncontrolled business, most likely, whose major concern is high profits. A hospital must adhere to rules and regulations of the State, unlike abortion clinics, they answer to no one for their mishaps, carelessness, or deaths that occur from having an induced abortion.

Abortion clinics are not required to have emergency-saving equipment. When there is an emergency, a woman must be transported to the nearest hospital. This can be crucial, especially when "time is of the essence" and a woman's life depends upon life-saving equipment and there is none.

After the abortion procedure a woman should have a follow-up examination, because this will insure her of a complete recovery, other wise, if a woman is bleeding internally, and has a hint of an infection, it can mean her recovery will be jeopardized, hospitalization and pos- sible surgery may be necessary, most importantly, it may mean a woman's survival. It is important for the woman to receive proper medication and/or treatment, because infection can escalate quickly, which could put the woman in danger of losing her life.

A follow-up examination, will also insure a woman from any possible life-long complication. If you choose to have an induced abortion, it is extremely important, it can't be emphasized enough how important that it is, that a woman has follow-up care.

As the aborted woman leaves the clinic, she should leave with a telephone number, to call 24 hours a day in case of an emergency. Also, she should leave the clinic, with a prescription for an antibiotic to protect the woman from possible infection. Plus, any other medications, to make the woman as comfortable as possible. She should, also, receive instructions, for postoperative care. And last, she should have a follow-up appointment, or a referral, for a checkup, within two to four weeks. T his follow-up visit, is to make sure the abortion is complete, and possibly discover and treat any complications that may occur.

Every woman is different, in their reaction to induced abortion, some women repress, or are unaware of any after effects, for years. Their reactions, may be delayed, but eventually will be triggered by some significant event, such as the birth of a child, the death of a loved one, or the end of a relationship, or a religious conversion. These are just a few events, that could present psychological problems for the aborted woman, and then, she may be in need of professional help. Unfortunately other children, in the family can be affected, by the mother's emotional problems, should she be afflicted with any. Also, the mother, who previously had an induced abortion, may have difficulty bonding to her other children. Or she may be overprotective.

In general, there are many other complications, deriving from having an abortion. One other major complication, is salt poisoning from the Saline Method (No. 4). This occurs when an excessive amount of salt is used to kill the unborn baby and gets into the mother's blood stream. It kills the unborn baby, however for the mother, some of backlash it causes, are headaches, terrible thirst, numbness, or tingling of the fingers, a sensation of burning up, also, convulsions that can lead to a coma. Salt poisoning is one of the most feared, potentially fatal complication. The mother's bladder could rupture, thereby becoming a life-long physical repercussion for her.

Furthermore, a possible embolism may occur. This is, when a substance, such as a blood clot, or any missed foreign object, like a piece of tissue, or even air, that may get into the mother's blood stream.. If this embolism is not discovered, it could wedge in some vital area where it may cause serious damage, thus, this mishap may require additional surgery, or once again, death, for the mother.

Should the Fallopian tube become damaged, it can lead to unexpeted involuntary infertility, meaning not fertile, unable to conceive, and have future children.

Another terrible possibility, is the fact, that the mother may suffer permanent brain damage, caused by the Saline Abortion (Method No. 4). Also, certain reactions, or side effects, occur to the mother when toxic drugs are given, to aid her, during the abortion procedure. These reactions, or side effects, are (1) shivering of the body, (2) difficulty in breathing, (3) shock and (4) possible total physical collapse.

Besides the possibility of perforation to the uterus, the mother's bladder, her bowels or abdomen, can be punctured. This can happen, because a great amount of force is needed, by the abortionist, when using the steel rods to get the cervix to expand, or to open up. This is not a good situation for the mother, remember, the cervix is not ready to expand at this time, because the birth cycle, is not complete.

The perforation of the cervix, is another problem and is on top of the list of complications, for the mother. Additional surgery may be required.

This is just the beginning of complications (remember there are over 100 complications), that could be inflicted, upon a woman, who chooses, to have an abortion. In one study, forty-three (43%) percent of deaths occurred, on the day of the abortion. That's almost one-half of the women who have an abortion. As previously mentioned induced abortion, is not the answer, for an unwanted pregnancy.

Another important issue that should be discussed and made available to women, is the length of time, between the beginning of an abortion and its completion. It is not publicized very much, for obvious reasons, but fact is, that women suffer hours of painful labor contractions, regardless of pain-killing medication given to them. They suffer from hunger (no food allowed during this time) and exhaustion, plus emotional stress. Also, during the abortion procedure, the female aborting is alone, and that, too, can be very stressful for her.

Doctors have known, for a long time, that people, are susceptible, to diseases of all kinds, when they are subjected to great stress. One negative event, such as an induced abortion, a death of a child, can cause enough distress, to lower the body's resistance to disease. Induced abortion is a experience of frustration, apprehension and fear, plus, it's a lonely time for the woman aborting. And for many women, it can become an experience ridden with guilt. Guilt is an extremely stressful condition, that could cause high blood pressure. High blood pressure or hypertension, alone, could influence other medical problems.

For example, some stress-related disorders are ulcers, cancer, hypertension, any of which, could lead to kidney damage, a stroke, inflammatory diseases of the colon and bowels, or respiratory disorders, such as asthma. Stress can also cause or aggravate many skin disorders.

Also, there are many complications that do not occur immediately, but may develop many years later, in the mother's future. One such complication, is cancer of her cervix, or breast cancer.

Sudden, unexpected change, from an ongoing pregnancy to a sudden end of child-bearing, can cause an imbalance of the woman's sensitive nervous system. A woman's reproductive organs and body have to wind down, to meet the consequences, of an unfinished pregnancy cycle. This may occur immediately, or as late in life, when a woman enters into menopause.

CHAPTER 6.

PSYCHOLOGICAL COMPLICATIONS

Some women are overwhelmed by negative feelings, such as fear of disapproval, or non-support, from the father of the child, parents and other family members, or friends, or even shame of their own choice to have an abortion. Some women may feel regret and anger. For many the reality of abortion is too painful to accept, leading a woman to deny and repress the facts of her experience. Rationalization and self-justification are common reactions, when a woman decides, to have an induced abortion.

One of the top after effects of having an induced abortion, is the psychological difficulty, that is felt by mothers, aborting their unborn babies, is feelings of 'guilt'. These feelings may create a depression, for the woman, that could last, as far in the future, as twenty-five years or more. She may never overcome this depression, without professional help

A change of attitude can occur in the woman after an abortion, about how she feels towards her sex partner. She may experience low self-esteem and feel worthless. This change of attitude may drive some women to drugs, or alcohol abuse, even suicide.

Some women may discover, that having a personal relationship, may be difficult to have, because induced abortion has, such an impact on a woman, physically and mentally. Also, emotionally.

Besides having communication difficulties, a woman may face the problem of becoming frigid. Re-occurring nightmares and insomnia, unable to sleep are other problems.

Induced abortion and breast cancer have been found to be connected. The rate of breast cancer, is rising rapidly, in many Coun-Tries, specially in the United States.

The first pregnancy, especially for a teenager, whose body functions or biological clock, that is interrupted, by an abortion, may end up with the worst complications. The most obvious changes are in the uterus or womb, but the rest of the body changes, especially the breasts. As pregnant women know, the breasts become tender and enlarged, to become a mature, milk-producing organ, in preparation, for the upcoming baby.

When a woman's body is violated, by induced abortion, it may provide a temporary remedy for the mother, by removing the baby from her body, however the hormonal changes, that are occurring inside of her body, have been interrupted. There is no way that can reverse the woman's body changes, caused by the pregnancy, therefore, these changes, make it more vulnerable, for cancer to manifest.

CHAPTER 7.

EMOTIONAL COMPLICATIONS

The physical scars, resulting from an abortion, will heal in time, but emotional scars do not heal as quickly, possibly never, without professional guidance. Why? Because induced abortion, is a violent, traumatic intrusion, imposed upon a woman's reproductive organs. The woman may feel relief when the abortion is over, but it is only temporary. Relief is then followed, by a period that psychiatrists identify, as emotional paralysis, or numbness, like a shell-shocked soldier. Most likely, these aborted women are unable, to express or feel their own emotions. Women, who, abort their babies, for health reasons, overcome emotional strife and cope with complications, arising from an induced abortion, much better.

Induced abortion will take its toll on women, especially teenagers. As before mentioned, a young girls' reproductive organs, are not yet fully mature, therefore induced abortion can be very damaging. It is more difficult to get the teenagers' cervix to dilate. Encountering this difficulty, the cervix, is prone to tears more readily. Therefore the young teenager, is more vulnerable and more susceptible to damage and complications, from having an induced abortion.

Post Abortion Syndrome (P.A.S) is known, as after-effects of abortion that many women suffer from. P.A.S. is a growing network of peer support groups of women, who are experiencing emotional difficulties. Women or family members, seeking help, can contact American Victims of Abortion at (202) 626-8800.

CHAPTER 8.

TEENAGE COMPLICATIONS

Teenage girls are under enormous peer social pressure, to have dates, which may lead to sex. If the teenage girl should, get pregnant, they may not realize they are pregnant, until they are well-advanced, into the pregnancy. Parental consent laws, sometimes, force pregnant teenagers, to hide their pregnancies, by causing them to make poor abortion decisions, or wrong choices. When they decide to have an abortion, it probably will happen in the second trimester of her pregnancy (trimester--3 months). No matter which trimester that a teenage girl has an abortion it will undoubtedly put her into a high risk position. One-fourth of all abortions, are performed on teens; most without their parent's knowledge or consent. One other obstacle they must contend with, is the cost of an abortion. The fee must be paid, up front, before the abortion is performed.

One very important reason why the risk factor is so high, is that the teenage girls' cervix is immature, or under developed. The cervix may be unable to dilate, even with drugs inducing dilation effectively. This results in an incomplete abortion. In this case, a second try at aborting the unborn is attempted, either by more drugs, or surgery.

For the teenage girl aborting, the percentage of success, is very slim. The possible problems that a young girl must face, may range from infections, hemorrhaging, hospitalization to additional surgery. The teenage girls are also strapped with intense physical pain, trauma, and the possible loss, of their reproductive organs, never to have a wanted baby in the future.

CHAPTER 9.

<u>WHEN AN ABORTION FAILS!</u>

Even a clinic with experienced and well-trained personnel, complications of incomplete induced abortions remain high in number. After the first attempt to have an abortion there are a number of women, for whom, a second attempt, also fails, then, surgical removal of the unborn baby is necessary. This presents several days of painful suffering, to an unanticipated, long hospital stay and not to mention the expense.

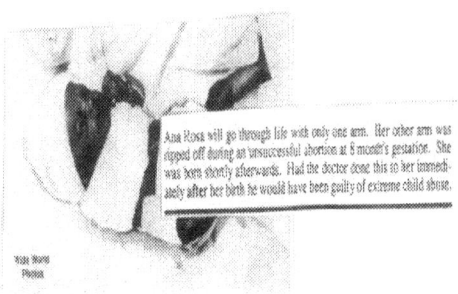

Ana Rosa will go through life with only one arm. Her other arm was ripped off during an unsuccessful abortion at 8 month's gestation. She was born shortly afterwards. Had the doctor done this to her immediately after her birth he would have been guilty of extreme child abuse.

As you can see from the picture illustrated induced abortions do fail, however, they do not fail to do their dastardly harm to the unborn babies, as well, as the mothers-to-be. When an abortion fails you wonder what could have went wrong. Abortion is supposed to be simple, safe and quick. That is what the abortion industry wants you to believe.

35

Unfortunately, this is probably the hardest time, for the woman aborting. She has to go through the abortion procedure again. There are no shortcuts. If the abortion fails again, then surgery is most likely in order. Each time a woman faces an abortion failure

This is especially difficult, for the teenage girl, life is just beginning for her, and she does not need these difficulties. If the teenager has no one to confide in, nor, given an opportunity to become informed, about the induced abortion that she is planning, a very heavy burden is placed on the teenage girl. They say 'ignorance is bliss', but not when you are having an induced abortion. Undoubtedly, teenage girls have many questions about an abortion and, if they go unanswered, by the professionals in the business, this may affect them mentally or emotionally. If the teenage girl had complete answers and/or full comprehension, of induced abortion, its procedures and the outcome of an induced abortion, as to its' many complications, she might considered other alternatives.

Any number of complications for the teenage girl could easily end up in her becoming sterile. She may have lavish dreams of the right man and wanted babies in her future life. However, becoming sterile can and will affect her the rest of her life. Young girls and women have been misled to believe that abortion, is the answer to birth control. Or a fast remedy for an unwanted pregnancy for whatever reason.

Abortion has been wrongly publicized. The biggest reason why that is, because induced abortion has become a highly profitable business. If many of the complications and the dangers of having an abortion, were publicized more, then, perhaps women would not accept induced abortion as readily. Women have become victims, because they have been led to think they can have a choice when it comes to their body. This is not true! A pregnant woman's choice may have been legalized, but women have not been properly informed, about all the complications. resulting from an induced abortion, nor, has the many deaths of mothers been publicly recorded.

Women who choose to have an induced abortion need to be thoroughly informed, as to all the possible complications, they may face, plus, the possible consequence of losing their lives. Women of all ages should become educated, as to exactly, how the female body, particularly, the reproductive system functions. Also, what could happen when the birth cycle is intruded upon, by having an induced abortion? Since there is no reverse apparatus to disengage, or to stop the birth cycle, complications are definitely, going to manifest, somewhere in the pregnant woman's body, either physically, menally or emotionally.

CHAPTER 10.

MEN AND ABORTION

What do some men see in induced abortion? In an extensive re-search, that was focused on abortion and women, it was reported, men have been legally, psychologically and medically, passed over. For men, the abortion issue, is a gnawing paradox, at a time, when some men are changing roles, and become increasingly involved with raising their children. In general, they are systematically denied, the right, to be involved in life-or-death decisions affecting their unborn children.

This powerlessness takes its toll, not only on the male self-image, but can bring on role conflict, excessive guilt, depression and, often, the end of the relationship, with his partner.

Abortion has been advocated, as a simple surgical procedure for women, which produces, little or no psychological impact for both sexual partners. This is not true, most men, as well as women, can not honestly, deny any negative emotional consequences from abortion.

Men who choose to accept their feelings, rather than deny them, often describe the abortion experience, as bewildering and painful, beyond their coping abilities.

It was reported, that three out of four male respondents studied, said "they had a difficult time with the abortion experience; they reported persistent day and night dreams about the child that never was, and considerable guilt, remorse and sadness".

For men and women alike, the feeling of emptiness may last a lifetime, for parents are parents forever, even of a dead child. Emotional resolution is nearly impossible, because there is no visible conclusion, just a memory. Because the unborn child was denied life, the child is denied a grave or marker. The grieving process is left unfinished.

If there is a lack of mutual agreement, between the partners, in the abortion decision, the ability to develop trust, communication, intimacy, honesty and companionship, is severely restricted. This same lack of mutual agreement will breed possible male aggression, which promotes child abuse, spousal abuse or self-abuse.

Clinical experience shows that men become hostile when they have been excluded, from decision-making, and when they discover they have been deceived and manipulated.

In the abortion decision, frequently, his sexual partner may not include him in the her decision to have an abortion, and is ignored at the abortion clinic. Also, he may feel helpless during or in the aftermath of the abortion itself. This conflict may be responsible for some of the increase in male sexual dysfunction

On the other hand, abandoning responsibility for men who don't care about the women they impregnate, abortion is a cool disposal system of the evidence of their sexuality. Becoming a father is far more responsible, than intercourse and conception.

When men promote abortion for their partners, it is classified, as coercion, lack of caring, insensitivity and selfishness. When women choose abortion, it is regarded as a woman's right.

Once the abortion has taken place, males may require as much **emotional support as females. For either sex, the loss of a child is a** loss like no other.

Abortion is a greater dilemma for men than is realized. Many men are victims, of abortion as well as, woman and unborn babies. With time, hopefully, humanity will realize that abortion is not a solution.

CHAPTER 11.

ARGUMENTS PRO AND.CON

When abortion became legalized in 1973, by the United States Supreme Court, in the case known as Roe -vs- Wade, it did not mean that abortion was safe. Legal does not have anything to do with safe. Since abortion is legal, a woman can get medical attention more readily without criminal investigation. All legalization of abortion did, was take abortion out of the back alley and put it in clinics. However, this was done, without restrictions, or thorough investigation to see how safe it was for a woman to have an abortion. No matter how good the doctor or abortionist is, the fact still remains you cannot interrupt, the natural process of the biological clock of child birth, without suffering the consequences of an unfinished birth cycle.

Another myth that is being promoted, is to mislead women into thinking that abortion procedures are simple and easier than child birth. Child birth has been in existence for eons, and with today's technology child birth, at any stage of the natural cycle, is safer than having an abortion. However, if a woman becomes pregnant, and still engages in harmful drugs, which includes alcohol, or in continued smoking of cigarettes, this certainly will affect the unborn baby making child birth unsafe.

An important question that should be answered is often avoided. If induced abortion is so safe and simple, why the lack of records being kept, in order to inform the public of its safety? Because, in reality, if actual figures, would become known, to the public, about the deaths and complications, that are derived from having an abortion, it would open women's eyes to see, by legalizing social abortion, that they are only being victimized, for profit, nothing more!

Abortion advocates should demand nationwide reporting to show that abortion is as safe, as they claim it is. Truthfully, it can't be done, because it is a fact, abortion is not safe. Yes, babies are dying in droves, but also, so are many mothers dying from having a legal induced abortion.

If women, who aborted, can overcome their embarrassment, shock, fear, and their grief, or feelings of guilt, they just may tell you just how devastating it really is. The bottom line is, if, they had the courage, they would tell you how alone you are at this time. It is a sad and tragic time, for women and teenagers, who undergo, the experience of having an induced abortion. You are alone, after all, it was your choice!

Then, there is the argument, of whether the unborn baby, is alive at the time of an abortion. The answer is yes, at the start of a heartbeat about 18 days from the time of conception. Another argument is, when is the unborn baby viable and should be considered a person with alienable rights? Some say an unborn baby has no rights, the mother, alone has the right, not the child.

Perhaps, knowing about genetics would be helpful. If the genetic pattern of any cell, of the mother's body were examined by a geneticist, surprisingly, it would be discovered that this pattern would be unique only to the mother. If the genetic pattern of any cell of the newly developed baby, were to be examined, by a geneticist, it would, also, be discovered that this pattern would be unique to the baby. The two genetic patterns of mother and baby, if compared, would most definitely, be different. Genetic patterns are as unique to individuals as a person's fingerprints.

The Constitution of the United States says "that all men are created equal". Then, it should be no matter, if it's a full grown person, or a baby in its' mother's womb. Therefore, according to the Constitution, all are created equal and are endowed with alienable rights. Surely a mother-to-be has a moral obligation, to protect her unborn child, whether viable or not, that is subjective to a violent act, such as an induced abortion.

QUESTION: "Why is a person charged with two counts of felony, when a pregnant woman is wrongfully killed?" Because a unborn baby is considered a separate life from the mother. The next question is, "Why do we have two standards of law in the country?"

ANOTHER QUESTION: "Why then does the clinician leave the unborn baby's head in the mother's uterus while the baby's life is taken? "The answer is simple, because once the baby is removed entirely, from the mother's body, takes its first breath, and then killed, it would classified as premeditative murder. Whether the head is left in the uterus or not, **MURDER IS MURDER!**

Illegal abortion was not safe, because a woman had to get an abortion in some back alley, or do it herself. She couldn't get medical attention, without being afraid of becoming involved, in a criminal investigation. But, once again, being legal does not make induced abortion safe, because induced abortion procedure, is still a traumatic invasion upon a women's body, while it is performing an uncontrollable natural function, known as child birth. Also, with abortion made legal, it has made it easier to pressure reluctant women, especially teenagers and young women into having induced abortions, it provides more profits for some, sadly, heartaches for others.

IN CONCLUSION, if you have decided to have an abortion prepare yourself for the worst. You will be putting your body on the line, no one else but you, remember it's your choice. No one can force you to do this!

As a result of having an induced abortion, there is a horrific amount of complications. One question, that should be answered is, "have these complications been suppressed, as not to scare women"? After all abortion is a business, and like any enterprise, profit is the main reason why they are in business. Every third woman that is pregnant will have an abortion. It is a profitable business indeed! The sadness of it is that getting these induced abortions are not just for health reasons, but too often abortion is just a means of birth control.

If women can get past the fact that induced abortion is horrible and if they can get over their embarrassment, their fear, their regret, shame or guilt, of having an abortion, then perhaps, abortion could be discussed openly. Particularly, how lethal it can be, and about the enormous amount of repercussions, that derive from having an induced abortion.

Too many young girls and women have been misled to think abortion is an answer to the dilemma of an unwanted pregnancy, and that it's a simple, safe technique and that it's a quick and easy remedy.

If you can become informed, as much as you can, about induced abortion, only this, will ultimately help you and others to make the right choice. A good place to start is your public library. Also, it would be excellent if schools would address induced abortion, as a subject matter.

Personal hygiene and sex are discussed, "why not include induced abortion and it's complications?" Maybe it is considered too emotional, to address abortion, as a subject matter. But knowing the depth of how an abortion can hurt a young girl, mentally, physically, and emotionally, there just might be less teenage pregnancies. Why not cover all bases, and learn about abortion and it's many complications?

Take time to learn all you can about induced abortion and what you may possibly have to face the rest of your life. Whatever you decide, decide for yourself, but with an open mind, that has been filled, with knowledge, about induced abortion, and its procedures. Plus, think about all the possible complications that could evolve from having an induced abortion. It would not be worth the unhappiness, that you might have to endure, for rest of your life, because of the choice you made. Women and young girls have been victimized long enough; they deserve to know the truth.

CHAPTER 12.

<u>GENERAL COMMENTS!</u>

The most important fact to remember, is that, you cannot disrupt the natural biological clock of child birth, without repercussions. A woman's body is a fine tuned instrument. When you stop a natural cycle from performing its function, which is a full term pregnancy, you put your body in a form of shock or suspension. The biological function of a woman's birth cycle only knows that a delay (by an abortion) was created. It is not programmed to stop and return the woman's body back to normal, before her pregnancy cycle is complete. The birth cycle cannot compute this sudden shock, and logically, there is no other alternative, but to malfunction.

When a woman is young and strong, who knows, how many years away this malfunction will take place. It could be as, far as when she enters menopause. It could be a physical malfunction, like cancer, or a mental or emotional one. All of which will require additional medical and/or psychological care. If your choice is to have an induced abortion, then, it should be a choice well thought out, and scrutinized with great care lest you become another victim of social abortion.

Now you may wonder why are toxic drugs, with such dangerous side effects, are being used, upon women, who wish to abort. One reason is, that the abortion and drug industry are making tons of money, millions, even billions of dollars from a woman's 'right to choose'. Abortion is the largest, uncontrolled industry in the United States.

Uncontrolled means that abortion providers, do not have to account to any one, nor do they have to keep records, true or otherwise, of how many actual women end up, with life-long complications, whether, they be physical, mental or emotional ones, or how many actual women have died from an induced abortion. There are questions that need to be answered by experts, who are honest and caring, and that aren't just interested, about the margin of profit made from induced abortions.

One controversy that plagues humanity is "when does life begin"? When a life has ended, a person is clinically dead, it is said their heart has stopped, and there is no pulse. Now logic would seem, if life ends with the stoppage of a heart beat, then why wouldn't life begin with a heart beat. So that means about 18 days from conception, a tiny heart starts to beat, so whether the unborn baby, is viable or not, it is alive.

According to the scientific community, the unique genetic pattern of each human being, is complete, from the moment of conception. This means, genetically speaking, at the time of conception, in one microscopic cell of the unborn baby, the baby has everything necessary to sustain life. Furthermore, nothing is added to this cell of the unborn baby, except protection and nourishment, that the baby receives from the mother. Nourishment is self-explanatory, but what about protection? What should protection include? Just what is a mother's function, is it not her loving duty to protect the rights of her child, whether, viable or not?

Since the Constitution of the United States, was written, that all men (women and children) are created equal, (from Webster's New World Dictionary, the meaning of the word 'create(d)' in part, means: "to cause to come into existence: bring into being"), and since the Constitution is meant to protect all persons, giving them certain alienable rights, among them the right to life, liberty and pursuit of happiness. You will notice that life is put before liberty and pursuit of happiness. It's up to the mother (and father) to protect the unborn baby's right to life. Apparently, life, whether it is a baby's life or a mothers, has very little value, all because a woman has been given a choice regarding her body. When in fact, the control of her body cannot be had, so she really doesn't have a choice.

Furthermore, the United States Supreme Court by making abortion legal, without prescribing rules and regulations, to follow, literally, gave abortion clinics a 'free hand' to operate as they chose. Unlike hospitals, abortion clinics, are not governed. In order to establish protection for women contemplating an induced abortion, is for legislatures (law makers) of this Country to petition, the Federal Court System, to enact laws protecting women. It should be the Court's responsibility to insure that women stop becoming victims through the illusion and misguided facts that, just because abortion was made legal by the court system does not make it safe.!

Consumer protection laws should be entered in the books and enforced. These consumer protection laws should include: 1) strict clinic regulations, i.e. to mandate emergency equipment be available; 2) informed consent requirement; 3) adequate waiting periods, and 4) public statistical data reporting complications, mishaps and deaths regarding results of women, from having induced abortions.

One avenue for a true and accurate way to know exactly how many women have encountered complications, due to having an induced abortion, is for a government agency, or a facsimile, to take a census from abortion recipients, and relatives or friends of women who have aborted and ended up with complications, or who have died.

Women should be fully informed and protected from the dangers having an abortion. On the surface, we know that induced abortion methods are lethal to unborn babies, so why should not women be informed, and made aware, of the dangers of an induced abortion to herself.

A short time ago in this country, it was a crime for a doctor to administer any foreign, toxic substance and/or the use of instruments, with the intention to murder a fetus, or unborn baby to procure a abortion on a woman who was with child. Also, a woman was executed if she partook in this crime.

Women in today's society have become victims of themselves, by allowing induced abortion practices to put them in a position where they think they have a choice.

In conclusion, the Hippocratic Oath, should be mentioned. It has been in existence for about 2,000 years, and been taken by physicians entering the practice of medicine. It is an oath where doctors have sworn and have given their word, that they will practice, the Profession of Medicine, with uprightness and honor. **In its original form, the so called Hippocratic Oath, prohibited a physician, to participate in abortion procedures.**

A question comes to mind. "What has 'having a choice', by legalizing abortion done to improve a women's life?". Answer: In all honesty, you could say, "absolutely nothing!"

CHAPTER 13.

IF YOU'VE BEEN INJURED BY ABORTION

PLEASE READ THE FOLLOWING!

These questions and/or commentary, were provided, by an established firm of lawyers, for their clients who may have fears and doubt about the abortion they had. These sample questions are designed to help you decide whether you should consider legal action against someone who might have injured you during an induced abortion.

These questions are as complete as possible, but they are just a guideline and should never be considered the last word on the subject. If the answers you give seem to indicate that you don't have justification for a lawsuit, but you're still not sure, please don't hesitate to seek a legal opinion.

The first thing you need to understand, is that simply being unhappy about your decision to have an induced abortion, is not justification for a lawsuit. The basic legal question is whether an injury occurred to you because of some action, or lack of action, on the part of the medical staff involved. Abortion may have been legalized, however, malpractice has not!

The following questions should help you determine whether that's the case. As you answer them, please keep in mind that your interest will be best served, by honest responses, which, neither minimize nor exaggerate, the facts about your situation.

QUESTIONS

1. Have you experienced any of the following problems since your induced abortion?

> Breast Cancer
> Liver Cancer
> Cervical Cancer
> Ovarian Cancer
> Endometrisis
> Uterine Perforation
> Cervical Lacerations
> Placenta Previa
> More irregular or heavier than
>   normal menstrual periods
> Chronic abdominal pain
> Gastro-Intestinal Disturbances
> RH Sensitization
> Pelvic Inflammatory Disease
> Other (specify)

2. If you were anesthetized during your induced abortion, did you experience complications due to the anesthesia? Yes No

3. Have you had problems conceiving a child since your induced abortion? Yes No

4. If you've been pregnant since your induced abortion, did you experience any of the following?

> Miscarriage
> Ectopic Pregnancy..
> Premature Delivery..
> C-Section
> Labor Complications
> Abnormal Placenta
> Other (specify)

5. If you had a baby since your induced abortion, was your baby born with any handicaps? Yes No

6. Since your induced abortion, have you experienced any of the following:

(a) a significant increase or decrease in your body weight; Yes No

(b) a significant increase in your use of alcohol, tobacco or drugs; Yes No

(c) a loss of pleasure from sexual relations; Yes No

(d) increased pain during sexual relations; Yes No

(e) an increase in self-destructive kinds of behavior (promiscuity); Yes No

(f) reckless disregard for your own well-being, thoughts of suicide, self-mutilation, etc.); Yes No

(g) a divorce or increased problems maintaining relationships with friends, relatives, boyfriends, co-workers, etc.; Yes No

(h) time periods during which your negative reactions to your abortion have made you unable to function normally in your work, home or personal relationships; Yes No

(i) a heightened dislike for all males; Yes No

(j) problems being abusive toward your other children, or toward any of your children born after the abortion; Yes No

(k) Other (specify).

7. Since your abortion, have you sought psychiatric counseling? Yes No

In the remaining questions, the term 'medical' staff refers to the person who performed your induced abortion, any counselor who visited with you, or any other employee of the facility where your induced abortion was performed.

The term 'referring agent' means any person or organization who, referred you to the facility where your induced abortion was performed. This could include a school councilor, a family planning organization (Planned Parenthood, Life Planning, etc.) a State Social Service or Welfare Agency, another physician, or anyone else whose actions might have caused you to patronize this particular abortion facility.

8. Did any member of the medical staff ever ask you if you'd had previous abortions? Yes No

9. Did any member of the medical staff take your medical history? For example, did they ask you if you were allergic to anything, had any prior surgeries, suffered from diabetes, etc.'? Yes No

10. Do you feel that the medical staff adequately informed you of the physical and/or emotional risks associated with having an abortion? Yes No

11. Do you feel that the medical staff gave you all the information you needed in order to make a fully informed decision to have an induced abortion? Yes No

12. Did the referring agent, or any member of the medical staff, ever suggest ways to cope with your crisis pregnancy situation which you now believe would have been better than induced abortion;(marriage counseling; adoption, etc.)? Yes No

13. Did any member of the medical staff suggest that an induced abortion was necessary in your case because of a medical condition which you now believe didn't exist? For example, did they tell you that you needed an abortion because your pregnancy was ectopic when, in fact they told you your unborn baby was handicapped although later information determined that it wasn't. Yes No

14. Do you feel that any member of the medical staff misled you about anything to do with your abortion decision, or the induced abortion procedure itself. Yes No

15. Did you indicate to the referring agent, or any member of the medical staff, that you were feeling pressured to have an induced abortion by someone else (husband, boyfriend, father, mother, friend, teacher, minister, etc.)? Yes   No

16. Was there ever a time when you felt you were being pressured to have an induced abortion by the referring agent, or any member of the medical staff? In other words, did it ever seem like they were trying to 'sell' you on the idea of having an induced abortion? For example, did they every say that abortion was cheaper than giving birth because of the expense of raising a child, or that having a baby could ruin your life? Yes No

17. Did you ever feel like you were being rushed into making the decision to have an induced abortion by the referring agent, or any member of the medical staff. For example, did they every say things like 'might as well get it over with,' or 'there's no time like the present, prices might go up next week'?   Yes No

18. Did you ask any member of the medical staff any questions about the decision to have an induced abortion, or about the abortion procedure itself, which they avoided or answered in a manner you feel was incomplete or inaccurate? Yes   No

19. Did you at any time indicate to the referring agent, or any member of the medical staff, that you were unsure about whether having an induced abortion was the right thing for you to do? Yes No

20. Did you at any time indicate to any member of the medical staff that you wanted to change your mind about having an induced abortion? Yes   No

21. Were you required to pay anything before you received counseling? Yes No

22. If you answered 'yes' to question 21, were you promised a refund if you changed your mind about having the induced abortions. Yes No

23. Did you ever ask the referring agent, or any member of the medical staff, to see fetal models or pictures which they didn't provide? Yes No

24. Did you ever ask any member of the medical staff any questions about fetal development which they avoided or answered in a manner you feel was incomplete or inaccurate? For example, did you ask them if induced abortion is the killing of a baby, or whether a baby feels pain during an abortion? Yes No

25. If you had a sonogram, did any member of the medical staff refuse to allow you to see the sonogram screen? Yes No

26. Have you learned information since your induced abortion that, had you known beforehand, might have caused you not to have the abortion? Yes No

27. Did the referring agent, or any member of the medical staff, ever suggest to you that induced abortion might be the right solution to your crisis pregnancy because of your age? For example, did they at any time suggest that you might be either too old or too young to have a baby? Yes No

28. Did the referring agent, or any member of the medical staff, ever suggest to you that induced abortion might be the right solution to your crisis pregnancy because of your financial status? For example, did they at any time suggest that you might be too poor to have a baby?   Yes   No

29. Did the referring agent, or any member of the medical staff, ever say anything that would suggest to you that they thought induced abortion might be the right solution to your crisis pregnancy because of your race or color?   Yes   No

30. While at the abortion clinic or doctor's office, were you ever the target of remarks, advances or suggestions of a sexual nature, or of touching that seemed inappropriate?   Yes   No

31. While at the abortion clinic or doctor's office. was there every anything said to you which you found insulting to you personally, or something which you might have taken as an insult to women.   Yes   No

32. Did the referring agent, or any member of the medical staff, ever have you sign a document which said that you would not hold them responsible if something went wrong during the induced abortion?   Yes   No

(NOTE: If you signed such a statement, be aware that it has no actual impact on your ability to seek compensation. You did not sign away your right to sue!)

The first section of questions (Numbers 1 through 7) were specifically designed to determine if and how you were injured. If you answered 'YES' to any of them you may have an injury that's actionable in court.

If that is so, the next thing to decide is whether negligence, incompetence, malice or any other wrongdoing on the part of the referring agent or medical staff contributed to the injuries you suffered. The second section of questions (Numbers 8 through 32) are intended to help make that determination.

If you answered 'NO' to Questions 8. 9, 10, 11, 12 or 22, or 'YES' to any of the other questions in this section, action taken by the referring, agent or the medical staff may have been contributing factors in your injuries.

WHAT NOW? First of all, please know that even if you don't have a basis for a lawsuit, you don't have to fight this battle alone. There are many dedicated organizations that offer free counseling to women who are hurting over their abortions.

On the other hand, if you now believe that you were in fact injured during your abortion, and if you, also feel that the medical personnel or the referring agent involved could have been at least partially responsible for those injuries, it may be time to talk to an attorney. Remember, whether you decide to seek help in a Court of Law, or in a Counselor's office, it's up to you to take the first step. Right or wrong, the healing process won't begin until you want it to!

Attorneys can help the many women who have become victims of induced abortion. By legal representation of these unfortunate women and/or their families, at this time, it will help them to understand that they have monetary recourse against whomever is responsible in regards to their personal tragedy.

Of course, nothing can undo a personal tragedy, but if the victimized woman and/or their families come forward and seek recourse in a court of law, then perhaps this notoriety will alert other women to the dangers of having an induced abortion.

NOTE FROM THE AUTHOR

I have tried to be nonbiased on the subject of induced abortion. But, in all honesty, I am against abortion, especially, if it is used as a social means, birth control, as a personal vendetta, or in a frivolous manner. I accept induced abortion, for health reasons, and if you personally chose to have an induced abortion, that is definitely your choice. All I suggest to you, is to think about the situation you are in, talk with someone to see what other alternatives there are, and investigate all the possibilities, of the many complications deriving from having an induced abortion.

An induced abortion may be the answer for you, right now, but it is a temporary solution. Abortion may provide temporary relief, from your pregnancy, but after an abortion, chances are, that the abortion, may generate a permanent and life-long complication.

THE BOTTOM LINE......

Today arguments still exist whether life begins at conception, or when the heart begins to beat, then there is the argument, whether the fetus is viable, or if a women has the right to govern her own body, by being able to choose to end her pregnancy, or not!

Many women are being injured over 100 different ways, from having an induced abortion, but are women aware of that. Is the seriousness, of having an abortion kept hush-hush, because the abortion industry has become such a lucrative, billion dollar business? Have women become victims for the legal right to be able to choose? Hopefully this book will help women, to understand the dangers, of having an induced abortion.

A biblical thought comes to mind, God said unto man and woman, "Go forth and multiply". It does not say, "Go forth and abort"!

Does a woman have the right to choose to end her pregnancy? According to man's law she has that right!

BUT WHAT ABOUT **GOD'S LAW,** SPECIFICALLY THE

FIFTH COMMANDMENT, which states,

"THOU SHALT NOT KILL."

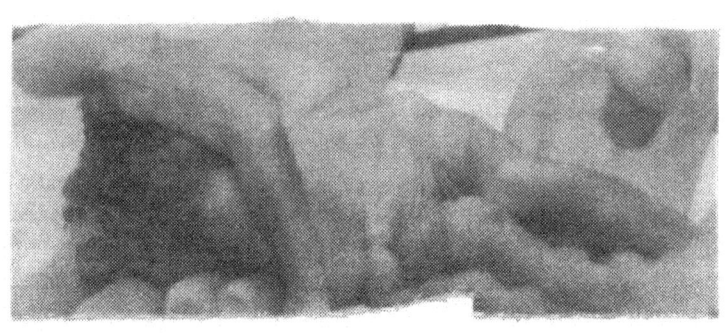